When you are a good helper,
it brightens everyone's day
because it makes things easier
for everyone!

Being a good helper
shows that you are growing up
and learning to do lots of things
all by yourself.
That makes you feel proud!

It's fun to be a helper and do your share.

Make it a Sunshine Day. Be a helper!

What should you do when you get to school?

You should hang up your coat
and put away your book bag.

Why?

Because putting away your things
shows that you are being a good helper
and that you can do it all by yourself!

What should you do during the day
when things get messy?

You should help clean up!

Why?

Because cleaning up messes shows that
you are being a good helper and doing
your share to keep everything tidy and clean!

What should you do when it's time to change
activities during the school day?

You should quickly finish what you are doing, clean up,
and get ready for the next activity.

Why?

Because moving quickly and willingly to the next
activity shows that you are being a good helper
by helping your class stay on schedule!

How should you play with
the books and toys at school?

You should handle them gently
and be careful not to damage or break them.

Why?

Because taking care of toys and books
shows that you are being a good helper
and doing your share
to keep everything in good condition.

What should you do if an adult
or classmate needs help?